D1470562

Disney's
WORLD OF
Riddles

by Oscar Weigle
and Tony Tallarico

Publishers · GROSSET & DUNLAP · New York
A FILMWAYS COMPANY

Library of Congress Catalog Card No. 78-71307
ISBN: 0-448-16827-8 (Trade Edition)
ISBN: 0-448-13127-7 (Library Edition)
Copyright © MCMLXXIX Walt Disney Productions.
World Wide Rights Reserved
Printed in the United States of America.
Published simultaneously in Canada.

When does a boat show affection?
When it hugs the shore.

What bird can be heard when you're eating?
A swallow.

What is the last thing Mickey Mouse takes off when he goes to bed?
His feet from the floor.

Who makes faces all day?
A worker in a clock factory.

What does Daisy Duck do when she stands on one leg?
She holds up the other one.

What works better when it has something in its eye?
A needle.

What kind of train chews bubble gum?
A chew-chew train.

**When Dumbo sits down on a chair,
what time is it?**

Time to get a new chair.

How do fishermen make their nets?
They take a handful of holes and sew them together.

If buttercups are yellow, what color are hiccups?
Burple.

If everyone owned a pink car, what would the country be called?
A pink car nation.

What's in an astronaut sandwich?
Launch meat.

How does a witch tell time?
With a witch watch.

What did one hot dog say to another?
"Hi, Frank!"

What did the robot say to the gasoline pump?

"Take your finger out of your ear and listen to me!"

Why is Pluto in an automobile like floor covering?

Because he is a car pet.

What do you do with a blue monster?
Cheer him up.

Where does a sheep get his hair cut?
At a baa-baa shop.

What is a liquid that can never freeze?
Hot water.

What is known as "brain food"?
Noodle soup.

Why wouldn't Goofy put coins in a pay telephone?
He believed in free speech.

What kind of pets make the best music?
Trum-pets!

If I had two hamburgers and you have two hamburgers, what would we have?
Lunch.

What is a HIbVE?

A small bee in a big hive.

What ghosts put out to sea?

The Ghost Guard.

What grows larger the more you take away?

A hole.

Where did Dopey try to find the English Channel?

On his TV set.

Why do farmers paint the inside of a chicken coop?

To keep the hens from picking the grain out of the wood.

How do you make a slow horse fast?
Don't give him anything to eat.

What do you call the last three hairs on Pluto's tail?
Dog hairs.

What is higher without a head than with a head?
A pillow.

What should you plant to make money?
Mint.

What's the difference between Pluto and a flea?

Pluto can have fleas, but a flea can't have Plutos.

Why did Goofy put one of his car wheels in his bed?
Because it was tired.

What always has an eye open but never sees?
A needle.

Why is the sun like a good loaf of bread?
Because it's light when it rises.

Why did Goofy take a bale of hay to bed?
To feed his nightmare.

How many balls of string would it take to reach the moon?
Only one—if it's long enough.

Why do birds fly south?
Because it's too far to walk.

Why do each of the 101 Dalmatians turn around several times before lying down?

Because one good turn deserves another.

What did the dirt say when it rained?

"If this keeps up, my name is mud."

If April showers bring May flowers, what do May flowers bring?

May flowers bring Pilgrims.

After the rain falls, when does it rise again?

In dew time.

Why do hens lay eggs only during the day?

Because at night they become roosters.

**Which player on a baseball team
wears the largest cap?**
 The one with the largest head.

**What was the name of the first
satellite to orbit the earth?**
 The moon.

**When does an Irish potato change
its nationality?**
 When it's French fried.

**What did the envelope say when it
was licked?**
 It just shut up and said nothing.

Where was Solomon's temple?
 On the side of his head.

Both Bambi and Thumper know how to hop and jump about. But what animal can jump as high as a tree?

Any animal. Trees can't jump.

What time spelled forward and backward is the same?

Noon.

Why did Goofy sleep in the fireplace?

Because he wanted to sleep like a log.

In what language should the last chapter of a book be written?

Finnish.

Why does Dumbo have a wrinkled skin?

Did you ever try to iron an elephant?

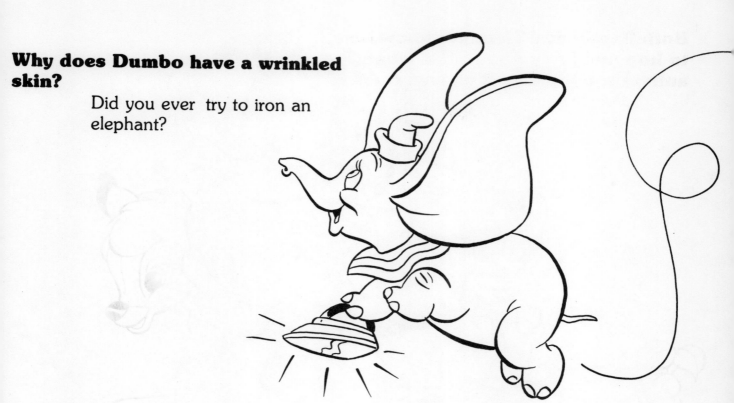

Why does Dumbo have his skin painted in many colors?

So he can hide in a jellybean jar. (If you have never seen Dumbo in a jellybean jar, you know how well it works!)

Why does Dumbo have a trunk?

He would look terribly silly with a glove compartment.

How does Dumbo get down from a tree?

He climbs out on a leaf and waits for fall.

Why can't Pinocchio's nose ever be twelve inches long?

If it were, it would be a foot.

What are the embers of a dying year?

November and December.

Why does the moon go to the bank?

To change quarters.

What makes the Tower of Pisa lean?

It never eats.

What bow can never be tied?

A rainbow.

What's the difference between a running man and a running dog?

The man wears trousers and the dog pants.

Minnie Mouse baked some cookies and sold them for 26¢ a dozen. How many could you buy for a cent and a quarter?

Twelve.

Why didn't Dopey shoo the flies?

He wanted them to stay barefoot.

What is the difference between a match and a cat?

A match lights on its head; a cat lights on its feet.

What's a cross between a dog and a chicken?

A pooched egg.

What did one candle ask the other candle?

"Are you going out tonight?"

What book has the most stirring chapters?

A cookbook.

How does one dinosaur tell another to hurry up?

"Pronto, 'Saurus!"

Where would Pluto go if he lost his tail?

To a retail store.

BONG BONG BONG BONG BONG BONG BONG BONG BONG BONG BONG BONG BONG BONG BONG

What time is it when the clock strikes thirteen?

Time to fix the clock.

Why do white sheep eat more than black ones?

There are more of them.

What is Kanga the Kangaroo's best year?

Leap year.

What will go up a chimney down, but won't go down a chimney up?
Mary Poppins' umbrella.

What is a wisecracker?
A smart cookie.

What did one wall say to the other wall?
"Meet you at the corner."

Where should a dressmaker do business?
On the outskirts of town.

Why do you make a mistake when you put on a shoe?
Because you put your foot in it.

What did the full-grown rose say to the little rose?
"Hi, ya, Bud!"

When is a car not an automobile?
When it turns into a garage.

Why can't a banana stay in the sun very long?

Because a banana peels.

Which month has 28 days in it?

They all have.

What speaks every language in the world?

An echo.

What do ghosts like to ride at amusement parks?

The roller ghoster.

When does a bed change size?
At night, when two feet are added
to it.

What is quicker than a fish?
Someone who can catch it.

**How can you always tell when a
train has left the station?**
It leaves its tracks behind.

What gives Mickey Mouse the power to see through walls?
Windows.

What is the most curious letter in the alphabet?
The letter Y.

What gets wetter and wetter, the more it dries?
A towel.

What does a mother fly do when her baby won't go to sleep?
She walks the ceiling with him.

When is a window like a star?
When it's a skylight.

How do you treat a pig with a sore throat?

Apply oinkment.

Why are prairies flat?

Because the sun "sets" on them every night.

When are eyes not eyes?

When the wind makes them water.

What is it that everybody in the world is doing at the same time?

Growing older.

Why should one expect to spend more money in the mountains than at the seashore?

Everything is higher in the mountains.

What's the difference between a counterfeit bill and an angry Thumper?

> One is bad money; the other is a mad bunny.

Why was Goofy using a steamroller on his farm?

> He was trying to raise mashed potatoes.

What can Clara Cluck break with her voice?

> Silence.

What kind of driver never gets arrested?

A screwdriver.

How do you make soup gold?

You put in fourteen carrots.

What did the tall chimney say to the short chimney?

"You're not big enough to smoke."

If an athlete gets tennis elbow, what does an astronaut get?

Missle toe.

Where were the first doughnuts fried?

In Greece.

What did Dumbo do when he stubbed his toe?

He called a toe truck.

What's gray, has four legs, and a trunk?

A mouse going on vacation.

On what day does Donald Duck talk the least?

December 21—it's the shortest day of the year.

What rolls around in mud and delivers painted eggs?
The Easter Piggy.

What can you give away and still keep?
A cold.

Where does a witch keep her spaceship?

In the broom closet.

What is the best day for making pancakes?

Fri-day.

Donald Duck doesn't dry dirty dishes. Can you spell that without using any D?

T-H-A-T.

Why does Goofy always carry a compass?
> So he'll know whether he's coming or going.

When is an operation funny?
> When it leaves the patient in stitches.

Why did Dumbo quit the circus?
> He got tired of working for peanuts.

What is the best way to talk to a gorilla?
> By long distance.

What did the fat man say when he sat down to eat?
> "I'm afraid all this food is going to waist."

Why didn't they play cards on Noah's Ark?
> Because Noah sat on the deck.

When a librarian goes fishing, what is used for bait?
> Bookworms.

Why did Goofy take a ladder to school?
> He wanted to go to high school.

Who is Snow White's brother?
Egg White. (Get the yolk?)

What is a volcano?
A mountain with hiccups.

What do you get when you cross an owl with an oyster?
An animal that drops pearls of wisdom.

How can you raise corned beef and cabbage?
With a knife and fork.

What tree does everyone carry in his own hand?
The palm.

How do you make notes of stone?
Just rearrange the letters.

When would a dog go to court?
When he gets a barking ticket.

What does Mickey Mouse say is the hardest part about learning to ice skate?

The ice.

What's the best way to catch a squirrel?

Climb a tree and act like a nut.

What is red and goes putt-putt-putt?

An outboard apple.

What do you call a monkey selling potato chips?

A chip monk.

What must Mickey Mouse know before teaching Pluto a trick?

More than Pluto.

Why is a baby like an old car?

They both have a rattle.

Why do witches ride brooms?
Because vacuum cleaners are too heavy.

What's the best way to keep Pluto off the street?
Put him in a barking lot.

If a farmer raises crops in dry weather, what does he raise in wet weather?
An umbrella.

What animal do you look like when you take a bath?

A little bear.

What is it that always goes around a button?

A goat. (A goat always goes around a-buttin'.)

What's the best thing to put in an ice cream soda?

A straw.

How did Pinocchio feel when the whale swallowed him?

He felt down in the mouth.

Why is Cinderella never on any baseball team?
Because she ran away from the ball.

Why is winter the best time to buy thermometers?

Because in summer they're
higher.

What do you call a sleeping bull?

A bulldozer.

How can you have a set of teeth inserted free?

Tease Pluto.

What words do you use to scold Dumbo?

"Tusk, tusk!"

What stays hot in the refrigerator?

Mustard.

What did one tube of glue say to the other tube of glue?

"We've got to stick together."

What time of year is it when a cat is about to pounce on a mouse?

Spring is coming.

Why did Goofy buy two ducks and a cow?

He wanted quackers and milk.

What is the biggest jewel in the world?

A baseball diamond.

What pine has the longest and sharpest needles?

The porcupine.

What sort of bed is a three-season bed?

One without a spring.

What starts with E, ends with E, and has one letter in it?

An envelope.

Why is baseball like cake?

Both need batters.

Where does Dumbo usually find peanuts?
The same place he left them.

What is the best kind of nut to eat when you have a cold?

Cashew.

Why is the center of a tree like Pluto's tail?

It's farthest from the bark.

Which weighs less, a full moon or a quarter moon?

A full moon is lighter.

What kind of fish can you find in a bird cage?

A perch.

Why is the letter A like a flower?

Because a "B" comes after it.

Why doesn't Goofy ever use toothpaste?

He says that his teeth aren't loose.

Why do weeping willows weep?

They are sorry for the pine trees that pine.

When painting a picture, what color would you use for the sun and wind?

The sun rose, the wind blue.

Why is it hard to talk with a goat around?

Because he always butts in.

What did the baby porcupine say when he backed into a cactus?

"Is that you, Ma?"

Why does the Statue of Liberty stand in New York Harbor?

Because she can't sit down.

Why is the Mad Hatter's tea party like a tennis game?

There is always a racket.

When is it right to serve milk in a saucer?

When feeding Figaro the cat.

What is a man called who steals ham?

A hamburglar.

Why is the sky so high?

So that birds won't bump their heads.

Why does Sleepy keep a clock under his pillow?

He likes to sleep overtime.

What is most useful when it is used up?

An umbrella.

Why did Goofy take a hammer to bed with him?

He wanted to hit the hay.

What do they call baby cats in Disneyland?

Kittens.

What is the best thing to put into a pie?

Your teeth.

What grows down while growing up?

Huey, Dewey, and Louie!

What is as light as air, yet even Dumbo can't hold it for ten minutes?

His breath.

Why is tennis such a noisy game?

Because each player raises a racket.

What bird can lift the heaviest weights?

The crane.

How can you leave the room with two legs and come back with six?

Bring a chair back with you.

What has many leaves, but no stem?

A book.

What is a daffy-down-dilly?

A crazy mixed-up pickle.

Why is a watermelon filled with water?

Because it's planted in the spring.

If you fed a cow money, what would you get?

Rich milk.

What did the cavemen eat?

Rock in roll.

What do you get when you cross a bumble bee and a school bus?

A humdinger.

What would boy and girl octopuses say to each other?

"I want to hold your hand, hand, hand, hand, hand, hand, hand, hand."

Why did the cookie cry?

Because his mother was a wafer so long.

Which is the left side of a blueberry pie?

The part that's not eaten.

What is the best way to find someone out?

Go to his home when he isn't in.

GONE FISHING

When does it cool off at a baseball game?

When there are lots of fans in the stands.

How can you live to be a hundred years old?

Eat an apple a day for 36,500 days.

Which one of the United States is a boat?

Ark.

When you lose something, why do you always find it in the last place you look?

Because you stop looking as soon as you find it.

Why is a pencil like a riddle?

Because it's no good without a point.

When should a baker stop making doughnuts?

When he gets tired of the hole business.

What's worse than raining cats and dogs?

Hailing taxis.

On which side does Donald Duck have the most feathers?

On the outside.

How can you make money fast?
Nail it to the floor.

What did the tie say to the hat?
"You go on a head—I'll just hang around."

Why is a large coat like a banana peel?
Both are easy to slip on.

What two animals go with you everywhere?
Your calves.

What has a big mouth but can't talk?
A jar.

What is a cocoon?

A wound-up caterpillar.

What's yellow and writes?

A ball-point banana.

What sort of wind comes after Lent?

An Easterly wind.

What's the difference between an old penny and a new dime?

Nine cents.

How do you make anti-freeze?

Take her blanket away.

Why are pins always getting lost?

Because they are pointed in one direction and headed in another.

What keys never open locks?

A mon-key, a don-key, and a tur-key.

What ring is best for a telephone?

Answer-ring.

Where does a jellyfish get its jelly?

From ocean currents.

Why doesn't the ocean overflow the land?

Because it is tide.

How many peas are there in a pint?
One p.

How can a leopard change his spots?

By moving.

What is sold by the yard and worn by the foot?

A carpet.

Why is Sunday the strongest day?
Because all the others are weekdays.

Why do people laugh up their sleeves?
Because that's where their funny bones are.

Why is it easier to clean a mirror than a window?
A mirror has only one side.

What's over your ear but under your hat?
Hair.

How far can Bambi run into the forest?

Only halfway. After that, he will be running out.

What's higher than a house and seems smaller than a mouse?

A star.

Why would a parrot carry an umbrella?

So he could be Polly-unsaturated.

How did Goofy get into his house when the door and windows were locked and he had lost his key?

He ran around and around until he was all in.

Why did Mickey Mouse make Pluto sit near the fire?

Because he wanted to have a hot dog.

When do ghosts have the most fun?

Whenever they're in high spirits.

What do you give a seasick lion?

Lots of room.

What does a cow become when it starts eating grass?

A lawn mooer.

When does it rain money?
Whenever there's some change
in the weather.

What is the difference between a hill and a pill?

One is hard to get up and the other is hard to get down.

Why are tall people the laziest?

Because they are longer in bed than short people.

Which animal is best at spelling?

A bee.

What goes zzub-zzub?

A bee flying backward.

Toot, whistle, plunk, and boom! What musical instrument never tells the truth?

A lyre.

How long will an eight-day clock run without winding?

It won't run at all without winding.

What runs over the pasture all day and sits in the refrigerator at night?

Milk.

What bet can never be won?

The alphabet.

When is a spanking like a hat?

When it is felt.

What do Eskimos call their cows?

Eskimoos.

How is it possible to have four hands?

By doubling your fists.

What does Donald Duck do when he flies upside-down?

He quacks up.

What do you call a dentist's office?

A filling station.

How do you make an apple turnover?

Tickle it under the stem.

When do Dalmatians have 404 legs?

When there are 101 of them.